Transformed
by the Jesus
presence of

CWR

Liz Babbs

Published 2012 by CWR, Waverley Abbey House, Waverley Lane, Farnham, Surrey GU9 8EP, UK.
Registered Charity No. 294387. Registered Limited Company No. 1990308. Reprinted 2013

Concept development, editing, design and production by CWR

Cover image: istock

Printed in England by Linney Print

ISBN: 978-1-85345-837-8

Contents

Introduction

Lent can be one of the richest times of the Christian year if we allow ourselves to enter into it fully. Preparing for Easter can be a time of spiritual refreshment and transformation.

People traditionally give up something for Lent, which is not a bad idea because the ability to fast from something means we are not controlled by it. However, I'd also like to encourage you to take up something this year and that is to spend more time 'hanging out' in Scripture, particularly the six passages I'm sharing with you in this book.

Transformed by the Presence of Jesus is an invitation to step inside Scripture to encounter Jesus through well-known characters in the Bible like Peter, Mary Magdalene, Lazarus and the Samaritan woman. Following the crucifixion, Jesus continued to touch and transform lives, making many resurrection appearances, including walking towards Peter on the water, meeting Mary Magdalene at the tomb, and talking with the disciples on the road to Emmaus. Many of these stories may already be very familiar, but, by spending more time engaging with them, God can give us new insights like fresh manna from heaven.

In addition to the more traditional Bible study approach with group discussion questions etc, I have woven into these studies the opportunity for personal and group reflection and meditation. At the end of each study I also invite you to try an imaginative meditation where you step into the Bible passage as though you were the Samaritan woman, or Peter walking on water. I have seen God work very powerfully through these meditations across the years. They work best using the audio tracks which I have voiced over music and these are available through my website: www.lizbabbs.com

Spending time in God's Word is an enriching experience. I have spent months and even years 'inside' some of the well-known passages that I'm sharing with you. The more I revisit them the more God speaks to me through them. And that process has helped me come to *know* Jesus, rather than know about Jesus,

as Paul explains so eloquently in Philippians 3:10 (Amp.):

> [For my determined purpose is] that I may know Him [that
> I may progressively become more deeply and intimately
> acquainted with Him, perceiving and recognising and
> understanding the wonders of His Person more strongly
> and more clearly], and that I may in that same way come to
> know the power outflowing from His resurrection [which it
> exerts over believers], and that I may so share His sufferings
> as to be continually transformed [in spirit into His likeness
> even] to His death, [in the hope] ...

And as we come to know Jesus, we also come to know God
because the Two are One.

The Easter message together with the traditional symbols
of the crucifixion and resurrection can easily become over
familiar. When a movie like Mel Gibson's *The Passion of the
Christ* is released or a work of art is commissioned, it can
allow us to see the Passion in new ways.

As I was researching for this book I came across a sculpture
of Jesus' crucifixion commissioned for the 400th anniversary of
the King James Bible called *Die Harder*, by artist David Mach.
The sculpture is constructed from 3,000 coat hangers and
depicts Christ crying out in anguish from the cross. The hooks
of the coat hangers have been straightened to form thousands
of spikes covering every part of His body. When interviewed,
David Mach explained that the reason he chose coat hangers
was because they are the most lowly and humble of materials.
And this is, of course, exactly what Jesus did. It was the most
lowly and humble individuals whom Jesus chose as His disciples
and promoted to positions of leadership. When I watched the
Royal Wedding, I loved the fact that the two people who had the
best seats next to William and Kate, were not celebrities, but two
nuns! God always promotes the humble.

Visiting Mach's sculpture at Southwark Cathedral was part
of my Easter pilgrimage. As I saw the sculpture in real life,
I was arrested by the pained beauty of Jesus and, as I sat for
several hours viewing it from different angles, it 'spoke' to me

in many ways. I knew that any pain I was experiencing now or in the future was nothing compared to the pain He suffered for me and the rest of the world. My pain, shame, guilt and sinfulness were pinned to the cross with Jesus and in their place was an open road – the road to freedom stretching all the way to eternity. How easy it is to take that freedom for granted.

Some visitors to the cathedral were shocked and revolted by the sculpture and said, 'How can this be the God of love?' But this *is* the God of love, because God showed the depths of His love for us through the barbaric crucifixion of His Son. It is 'beauty' rising from the ashes of suffering borne for the sake of the whole world. Jesus has taken the barbs of injustice, abuse, violence and slander. No matter what we go through or to what depths we plummet, His suffering releases us because He has gone ahead of us. And the resurrection demonstrates the sheer persistence of God's love. God is totally committed to being our God forever, having given us the priceless gift of victory over death.

In *Transformed by the Presence of Jesus*, as I share Jesus' life-changing power to transform a person forever, my prayer is that God will reveal more of Himself to you through the rich treasure of His Word and your faith will deepen to such a degree that you, like Peter, will begin water-walking!

Jesus
The Word made flesh
A new translation
Born into time and space
A fresh revelation.

Walks the earth
in moving meditation.
Delivering
Healing
Releasing
from condemnation.

© Liz Babbs

Walking with Jesus
Luke 24:13-35

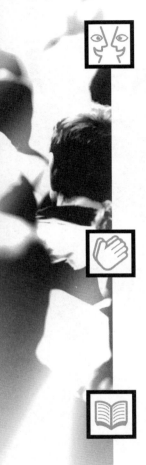

Icebreaker

How do you see your year developing from this point onwards? Is there a picture, image or word that describes it? If you were to imagine your walk with God visually, what would it look like? Is it a flat line with a few undulations? Is it a straight line or a meandering course? Or is it a steep incline or descent? Are there any road blocks or diversions? Or does your life seem more like a roller coaster?

Pray first and then make a simple line drawing. You may want to consider my own example found on my website: www.lizbabbs.com

Opening Prayer

Lord, we come to You, longing to know You better in the twists and turns, the ups and downs, of our lives. Lord, please reveal Yourself to us even in those times when we seem to hit a dead end or our very foundations are shaken. Help us to trust in Your leading – even when the road seems dark and uncertain. Speak to us Lord and open Your Word to us, in Jesus' name. Amen.

Bible Readings

Genesis 5:22
... Enoch walked with God 300 years ...

Genesis 6:9
Noah was a righteous man, blameless among the people of his time, and he walked with God.

Genesis 17:1–2
When Abram was ninety-nine years old, the Lord appeared to him and said, 'I am God Almighty; walk before me and be blameless. I will confirm my covenant between me and you and will greatly increase your numbers.'

Micah 6:8
And what does the Lord require of you?

To act justly and to love mercy
and to walk humbly with your God.

Eye Opener

Have you ever been the wrong way around a one-way system?
I have when I visited IKEA. Well, I couldn't be bothered to go
all the way round their long one-way system just to pick up an
item that was nearer the exit than the entrance of the shop. So,
I decided to enter the exit! As I proceeded, I was met with lots
of shopping trolleys hurtling towards me. I was exasperated
as I wove my way in and out of them. But I had no right to be
angry, I was at fault. I had decided to go against the flow and
was suffering the consequences. What did I expect?

As Christians we are called to be counter cultural – to
go against the cultural flow – and it is very uncomfortable
at times. Christians are in the minority, called to be in the
world, but not of it. But it is God we are meant to walk in
step with, not our culture. The natural tendency is to do what
others are doing, but Christians need to stand firm and resist
ungodly trends.

Setting the Scene

It was the day of the resurrection, and two of Jesus' disciples were
walking from Jerusalem to Emmaus having witnessed Jesus'
execution. They were thoroughly disillusioned. They had been full
of hope and expectation, but now all hope seemed gone, because
they had not yet heard the good news of Jesus' resurrection.

They believed they had lost Jesus, the person who meant
everything to them, having seen His violent, degrading death on
the cross. Jesus, their friend, had been made a public spectacle;
He had been jeered at and flogged. Naturally, they were shell-
shocked – traumatised by the violence they had witnessed.

Just a week earlier things had been so different as Jesus
entered Jerusalem riding on a donkey, palm branches waving in
celebration. But now all joy was gone. The stark reality hit home:
'... we had hoped that he was the one who was going to redeem

Israel', they remarked' (v.21). But their master was incarcerated in a tomb. The Light of the world had gone out.

Session Focus

Relax, close your eyes and come on a journey along the road to Emmaus.

As you listen to the passage of Scripture read to you several times, see if any words or sentences stand out or become highlighted in some way. At the end of the readings, spend a couple of minutes in silence asking God to show you what He might be saying to you through any words, thoughts or images that drop into your mind. Then, discuss your thoughts with your group. Alternatively, if you're studying this book independently, why not use the opportunity to record your thoughts in a journal?

On the Road to Emmaus (Luke 24:13–35)

Now that same day two of them were going to a village called Emmaus, about seven miles from Jerusalem. They were talking with each other about everything that had happened. As they talked and discussed these things with each other, Jesus himself came up and walked along with them; but they were kept from recognising him.

He asked them, 'What are you discussing together as you walk along?'They stood still, their faces downcast. One of them, named Cleopas, asked him, 'Are you only a visitor to Jerusalem and do not know the things that have happened there in these days?'

'What things?' he asked.

'About Jesus of Nazareth,' they replied. 'He was a prophet, powerful in word and deed before God and all the people. The chief priests and our rulers handed him over to be sentenced to death, and they crucified him; but we had hoped that he was the one who was going to redeem Israel. And what is more, it is the third day since all this took place. In addition, some of our women amazed us. They went to the tomb early this morning but didn't find his body. They came and told us that they had seen a vision of angels, who said he was alive. Then some of our companions went to the tomb and found it just as the women had said, but him they did not see.'

He said to them, 'How foolish you are, and how slow of heart to believe all that the prophets have spoken! Did not the Christ have to suffer these things and then enter his glory?' And beginning with Moses and all the Prophets, he explained to them what was said in all the Scriptures concerning himself.

As they approached the village to which they were going, Jesus acted as if he were going further. But they urged him strongly, 'Stay with us, for it is nearly evening; the day is almost over.' So he went in to stay with them.

When he was at the table with them, he took bread, gave thanks, broke it and began to give it to them. Then their eyes were opened and they recognised him, and he disappeared from their sight. They asked each other, 'Were not our hearts burning within us while he talked with us on the road and opened the Scriptures to us?'

They got up and returned at once to Jerusalem. There they found the Eleven and those with them, assembled together and saying, 'It is true! The Lord has risen and has appeared to Simon.' Then the two told what had happened on the way, and how Jesus was recognised by them when he broke the bread.

Discussion Starters

1. What do you think 'walking with God' means or looks like?

_____

_____

_____

_____

_____

2. How might history have been different if Adam had 'walked with God'?

_____

_____

_____

_____

_____

3. Why was only one of the disciples, Cleopas, named?

_____

_____

_____

_____

_____

4. Are there any areas in your life where you 'had hoped' that God would answer your prayers, but He hasn't yet?

_____

_____

_____

_____

_____

5. How do you understand hope?

_____

_____

_____

_____

_____

6. Have you ever felt as if you were in darkness?

_____

_____

_____

_____

_____

7. Some people pour out their hearts to God through a letter, prayer, poem or journal; while others 'chat' away in their cars or when they go for a walk or a jog. How and where do you like talking to God?

_____

_____

_____

_____

_____

8. 'When he was at the table with them, he took bread, gave thanks, broke it and began to give it to them. Then their eyes were opened and they recognised him, and he disappeared from their sight' (Luke 24:30–31). When did Jesus become real to you?

_____

_____

_____

_____

_____

Final Thoughts

Talking is an important part of processing feelings. So, when a stranger joined them on the road, the disciples poured out their hearts to Him. This would be the most important walk of their lives. Jesus offered His disciples unconditional love and a time of intimacy when they could share their vulnerability and pain. He had not abandoned them. Quite the opposite, He was with them, opening their understanding to the Scriptures along the way. They had assumed that the Messiah would come with power and glory to strike down their enemies, but Jesus explained to them that His death was part of God's plan of salvation.

We have a Saviour who walks alongside us. We don't walk alone, however long and lonely the journey may seem at times. Sometimes we may run ahead or lag behind, but in time we learn how to walk at God's speed. We learn to stay close enough to hear the leading of His 'still small voice'.

Intimacy is about sharing the deepest part of ourselves with God. Often we put up walls because such transparency can be uncomfortable, but intimacy is about sharing vulnerability, love and trust. Jesus went to hell and back to give us intimacy with the Father. It was His ultimate gift – shared for all humankind. It was during the intimacy of a shared meal when Jesus broke bread and gave thanks, that the disciples recognised Him.

As soon as the disciples recognise the identity of the stranger He vanishes. This might seem like the stuff of fairy tales, but this is Jesus. He had revealed Himself to the disciples, given them 'hope and a future' (Jer. 29:11); now it was time for them to live and walk out that hope in His magnificent presence. God continues to give us glimpses of Himself across our lives, enough to sustain us and keep our faith strong on the journey.

Closing Prayer

Lord, thank You for the invitation to walk with You that was bought with such a price. Thank You that You extend that invitation daily. For You created us for Yourself, and our hearts are restless until they find their home in You. Amen.

Further Reflection

The Emmaus Road – Imaginative Meditation

Take your time to pause in between the questions and sentences below, or use my recording of 'The Emmaus Road'. This imaginative meditation voiced over music is available from my website: **www.lizbabbs.com**

I'd like to invite you to step into the Bible story where Jesus walks alongside the disciples on the Emmaus Road. You might like to imagine yourself walking with Jesus in a location that's familiar to you.

Imagine yourself walking in that location now ...

What can you see?

Can you hear anything?

What are you feeling?

How fast are you walking?

Now imagine Jesus walking alongside you.

Is He on your right or your left?

How fast are you walking now?

Is Jesus saying anything to you?

What is Jesus doing?

And are you saying anything to Jesus?

And how does this special time with Jesus end?

Known by Jesus
John 4:1-26

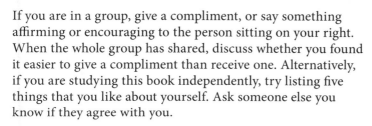

Icebreaker

If you are in a group, give a compliment, or say something affirming or encouraging to the person sitting on your right. When the whole group has shared, discuss whether you found it easier to give a compliment than receive one. Alternatively, if you are studying this book independently, try listing five things that you like about yourself. Ask someone else you know if they agree with you.

Opening Prayer

Father God, thank You that we are fully known by You. You know us, better even than we know ourselves. Soften our hearts so that we might allow Your love to penetrate deeper. Help us to seek our worth and acceptance in You alone so that we can live and worship freely in the way You created us to. Amen.

Eye Opener

Have you ever queued up to meet somebody famous? I have. On a couple of occasions I have waited outside the theatre at the Stage Door to get an autograph from a celebrity. As a balletomane, I have queued to meet Nureyev, Margot Fonteyn and Baryshnikov. More recently I queued for an hour to meet my comedy heroes, French and Saunders. Now I may have met French and Saunders and watched most of their comedy shows, but I don't 'know' them.

Likewise, the readers of my books often say, 'Liz, I feel like I know you.' But they don't really 'know' me. They only know the parts of me that I choose to reveal in my books. Only a couple of people know me really well, but even they don't know me like God does.

I love the fact that we are known by God and in that knowing are welcomed, accepted and cherished by Him. God knows us in ways no one else can, because He created us – and that knowledge releases us into the freedom of experiencing life in all its fullness (John 10:10). But I sometimes wonder, how many of us truly experience the fullness of that freedom that Jesus bought for us.

Bible Readings

Jeremiah 1:5
Before I formed you in the womb I knew you,
before you were born I set you apart ...

John 10:14,27
I am the good shepherd; I know my sheep
and my sheep know me ...
My sheep listen to my voice; I know them,
and they follow me.

Jeremiah 31:3 (NLT)
... I have loved you, my people, with an everlasting love.
With unfailing love I have drawn you to myself.

1 Peter 2:9-10 (The Message)
But you are the ones chosen by God, chosen for the high calling of priestly work, chosen to be a holy people, God's instruments to do his work and speak out for him, to tell others of the night-and-day difference he made for you – from nothing to something, from rejected to accepted.

1 Corinthians 8:3 (TNIV)
But whoever loves God is known by God.

Psalm 139:1-3,13-14
O LORD, you have searched me
and you know me.
You know when I sit and when I rise;
you perceive my thoughts from afar.
You discern my going out and my lying down;
you are familiar with all my ways ...
For you created my inmost being;
you knit me together in my mother's womb.
I praise you because I am fearfully and wonderfully made;
your works are wonderful,
I know that full well.

Setting the Scene

Jesus was on His way to Galilee and decided to take a shorter route via the village of Sychar. He was tired and thirsty, so He sat for a while at Jacob's well which was near Mount Gerizim, the site of the Samaritan temple, Samaria's holy place. The well was on the property originally owned by Jacob, located just outside the city. Here Jesus met a Samaritan woman and asked her for a drink. Women did not normally draw water from wells at noon and it is possible she chose this time to avoid meeting people because she had a questionable reputation.

Talking to a woman and a Samaritan broke many Jewish customs, because the Jews traditionally despised the Samaritans and men did not speak to women during those times. But Jesus not only spoke to the Samaritan woman, He initiated the conversation, asking her for a drink of water – thereby crossing all social and religious boundaries to share the gospel with her.

Jesus was no people-pleaser. We see Him throughout the Gospels eating, drinking and ministering to people who would have been considered social outcasts. The fact that Jesus knew everything about the Samaritan woman signalled to her that He was her Messiah.

Session Focus

Relax, close your eyes and come and meet Jesus at the well.

As you listen to the passage of Scripture read to you several times, see if any words or sentences stand out or become highlighted in some way. At the end of the readings, spend a couple of minutes in silence asking God to show you what He might be saying to you through any words, thoughts or images that drop into your mind. Then discuss your thoughts with your group or take time to record them for your own personal reflection.

Jesus Talks With a Samaritan Woman (John 4:1-26)

The Pharisees heard that Jesus was gaining and baptising more disciples than John, although in fact it was not Jesus who baptised, but his disciples. When the Lord learned of this, he left Judea and went back once more to Galilee.

Now he had to go through Samaria. So he came to a town in Samaria called Sychar, near the plot of ground Jacob had given to his son Joseph. Jacob's well was there, and Jesus, tired as he was from the journey, sat down by the well. It was about the sixth hour.

When a Samaritan woman came to draw water, Jesus said to her, 'Will you give me a drink?' (His disciples had gone into the town to buy food.)

The Samaritan woman said to him, 'You are a Jew and I am a Samaritan woman. How can you ask me for a drink?' (For Jews do not associate with Samaritans.)

Jesus answered her, 'If you knew the gift of God and who it is that asks you for a drink, you would have asked him and he would have given you living water.'

'Sir,' the woman said, 'you have nothing to draw with and the well is deep. Where can you get this living water? Are you greater than our father Jacob, who gave us the well and drank from it himself, as did also his sons and his flocks and herds?'

Jesus answered, 'Everyone who drinks this water will be thirsty again, but whoever drinks the water I give him will never thirst. Indeed, the water I give him will become in him a spring of water welling up to eternal life.'

The woman said to him, 'Sir, give me this water so that I won't get thirsty and have to keep coming here to draw water.'

He told her, 'Go, call your husband and come back.'

'I have no husband,' she replied.

Jesus said to her, 'You are right when you say you have no husband. The fact is, you have had five husbands, and the man you now have is not your husband. What you have just said is quite true.'

'Sir,' the woman said, 'I can see that you are a prophet. Our fathers worshiped on this mountain, but you Jews claim that the place where we must worship is in Jerusalem.'

Jesus declared, 'Believe me, woman, a time is coming when you will worship the Father neither on this mountain nor in Jerusalem. You Samaritans worship what you do not know; we worship what we do know, for salvation is from the Jews. Yet a time is coming and has now come when the true worshipers will worship the Father in spirit and truth, for they are the kind of worshipers the Father seeks. God is spirit, and his worshipers must worship in spirit and in truth.'

The woman said, 'I know that Messiah' (called Christ) 'is coming. When he comes, he will explain everything to us.'

Then Jesus declared, 'I who speak to you am he.'

Discussion Starters

1. What do you think might have compelled Jesus to travel through Samaria? Was it a deliberate choice or just part of the route to Galilee?

_____

_____

_____

_____

_____

2. How did Jesus treat the Samaritan woman?

_____

_____

_____

_____

_____

3. How accepted do you feel by Jesus? Try and give it a number on a scale of 1 to 10, where '10' indicates fully accepted and '1' indicates hardly accepted.

1	2	3	4	5	6	7	8	9	10

4. What does it mean to worship 'in spirit and in truth' (v.23)?

_____

_____

_____

_____

_____

5. What did Jesus mean by 'living water' (v.10)?

_____

_____

_____

_____

_____

6. What do you need God to fill you with today?

_____

_____

_____

_____

_____

7. In what ways have you shared your experience of Jesus with someone?

_____

_____

_____

_____

_____

8. Lent can be a season of pruning and letting go. Are there any things in your life you'd like to change as you walk with God through Lent this year?

_____

_____

_____

_____

_____

Final Thoughts

The woman took the risk of coming to the well to fill her jar. She had no idea that this particular day would change the rest of her life, or that her testimony would affect a whole village. She was empty like her jar, but left the well full of living water, having met the Messiah. No wonder she forgot her jar. Little did she realise that from this day on she would never thirst again. And after her life-changing encounter with Jesus, she ran to tell the people in her town. The living waters were already bubbling up and flowing out through her to others.

Initially the woman misunderstood what Jesus meant about living water. She thought Jesus was talking about a way that would save her visiting the well. It was obviously going to take her some time to understand the significance of this encounter because it shook her very foundations. If the Queen of England were to pay you a personal visit, you might be in shock for several hours and it might take several days to realise that you had actually met her! Well Jesus, the King of kings, chose to spend time with this Samaritan woman of questionable repute. No wonder she was in shock!

Emphasis is often placed on the importance of us knowing God, but we can only know God because we are first known by Him. Isn't it wonderful to think that God knows us so intimately that He has written our names on the palm of His hand (Isa. 49:16) and every hair on our head is numbered (Matt. 10:30)? We are forever on God's mind and there is no moment when His care falters. God so values our friendship He was willing to sacrifice His Son for it – which makes our friendship with Him priceless.

Closing Prayer

Lord, we thank You that through Jesus, sin no longer separates us from Your love. Lord, we come to You longing to know the fullness of Your acceptance of us. Continue to make Your love known to us and help us receive that love every day of our lives. Amen.

Further Reflection

The Woman at the Well – Imaginative Meditation

Take your time to pause in between the questions and sentences below, or use my recording of 'The Woman at the Well'. This imaginative meditation voiced over music is available from my website: **www.lizbabbs.com**

I'd like to invite you to step into the Bible story where Jesus talks to the Samaritan woman at the well.

Imagine yourself sitting at the well with Jesus now, just enjoying His company.

Is Jesus sitting on your right or your left?

What does He look like?

What is He wearing? What are you wearing?

What is the expression on Jesus' face?

How are you feeling?

Is there anything you want to say to Jesus?

What is He saying to you?

Now if you're aware of any worries or anxieties, you might want to talk to Jesus about these and hand over your concerns to Him. And just as the woman at the well left her water jar there, you might want to leave your worries with Jesus.

And now just relax and enjoy resting in God's presence.

Waiting for Jesus
John 11:1-44

Icebreaker

(See Leader's Notes.)

Opening Prayer

Lord, there may be many things that bind us and prevent us from experiencing a deeper relationship with You. We pray that You would reveal these areas to us and help us to yield our hearts more fully to You. Amen.

Bible verses

Psalm 62:5-6

Find rest, O my soul, in God alone;
my hope comes from him.
He alone is my rock and my salvation;
he is my fortress, I will not be shaken.

Hosea 12:6 (NASB)

Therefore, return to your God,
Observe kindness and justice,
And wait for your God continually.

Isaiah 40:31 (NASB)

Yet those who wait for the LORD
Will gain new strength;
They will mount up *with* wings like eagles,
They will run and not get tired,
They will walk and not become weary.

Psalm 27:14

Wait for the LORD;
be strong and take heart
and wait for the LORD.

Lamentations 3:25 (NASB)

The LORD is good to those who wait for Him,
To the person who seeks Him.

John 14:27 (Amp)

Peace I leave with you; My [own] peace I now give *and*
bequeath to you. Not as the world gives do I give to you.

Do not let your hearts be troubled, neither let them
be afraid. [Stop allowing yourselves to be agitated and
disturbed; and do not permit yourselves to be fearful and
intimidated and cowardly and unsettled.]

Isaiah 64:4

Since ancient times no one has heard,
no ear has perceived,
no eye has seen any God besides you,
who acts on behalf of those who wait for him.

Proverbs 8:34 (TNIV)

Blessed are those who listen to me,
watching daily at my doors,
waiting at my doorway.

Eye Opener

I don't know about you, but I'm not naturally a patient person.
I don't like waiting and become easily annoyed by long queues,
especially ones that don't move forward. Recently, I tried to
challenge my levels of patience by deliberately choosing the
longest queues at supermarket check outs and then, instead of
getting agitated, I prayed for all the people in front and behind
me. I tried this in traffic queues too. But boy, was it a tough habit
to cultivate! Patience is a fruit of the Spirit which takes time to
grow and I clearly need more practice developing this fruit!

Sometimes, waiting for God to answer my prayers tests my
patience too. But it also stretches my faith. No wonder the
psalmists repeatedly ask God, 'How long?' But, while I wait
for God I am growing in God, so the waiting is not a waste of
time, but an investment of time.

Setting the Scene

Mary and Martha lived in Bethany, a village near Jerusalem,
where Jesus often lodged when He came up to the feasts.
Jesus felt at home with His good friends Mary, Martha and
Lazarus – it was like His home away from home.

On this occasion though, things were dire. Their brother was

dying and so the sisters sent word to Jesus. But Jesus makes them wait – and not just for a few hours, but for several days! I feel sorry for Mary and Martha because the waiting must have been excruciating. Jesus, the Great Physician, seems to have abandoned His friends in their time of greatest need. I doubt He was caught in a traffic jam on His way to Bethany, so He must have had another agenda – His Father's. A greater miracle would be manifested as a result of this delay which would point to the resurrection of hope for all humankind. But at the time Mary and Martha did not know that.

Jesus knew how to wait. He was not driven by the crisis of the moment, other people's agendas or the expectations of the culture. 'My food' said Jesus, 'is to do the will of him who sent me and to finish his work' (John 4:34).

In this story, Jesus also displays His humanity and He weeps. Mary and Martha were distraught, and Jesus is agitated even though He had assured them that, 'This sickness is not fatal. It will become an occasion to show God's glory by glorifying God's Son' (v.4). In other words, there is a purpose to Lazarus' sickness. Jesus expressed Himself clearly but Mary and Martha do not understand what He means. There's even a comic moment of misunderstanding when the disciples remark of Lazarus, 'Master, if he's gone to sleep, he'll get a good rest and wake up feeling fine' (v.12). I wonder whether Jesus' anger in this story might have been the frustration He felt that even His closest friends didn't fully recognise Him as the Messiah.

Session Focus

Relax, close your eyes and come on a journey to meet Mary, Martha and Lazarus as they wait for Jesus. As you hear this passage of Scripture read to you several times, see if any words or sentences stand out or become highlighted in some way. At the end of the readings, spend a couple of minutes in silence asking God to show you what He might be saying to you through any words, thoughts or images that drop into your mind. Then discuss your thoughts with your group or take time to record them for your own personal reflection.

The Death of Lazarus (John 11:1-44, The Message)

A man was sick, Lazarus of Bethany, the town of Mary and her sister Martha. This was the same Mary who massaged the Lord's feet with aromatic oils and then wiped them with her hair. It was her brother Lazarus who was sick. So the sisters sent word to Jesus, 'Master, the one you love so very much is sick.'

When Jesus got the message, he said, 'This sickness is not fatal. It will become an occasion to show God's glory by glorifying God's Son.'

Jesus loved Martha and her sister and Lazarus, but oddly, when he heard that Lazarus was sick, he stayed on where he was for two more days. After the two days, he said to his disciples, 'Let's go back to Judea.'

They said, 'Rabbi, you can't do that. The Jews are out to kill you, and you're going back?'

Jesus replied, 'Are there not twelve hours of daylight? Anyone who walks in daylight doesn't stumble because there's plenty of light from the sun. Walking at night, he might very well stumble because he can't see where he's going.'

He said these things, and then announced, 'Our friend Lazarus has fallen asleep. I'm going to wake him up.'

The disciples said, 'Master, if he's gone to sleep, he'll get a good rest and wake up feeling fine.' Jesus was talking about death, while his disciples thought he was talking about taking a nap.

Then Jesus became explicit: 'Lazarus died. And I am glad for your sakes that I wasn't there. You're about to be given new grounds for believing. Now let's go to him.'

That's when Thomas, the one called the Twin, said to his companions, 'Come along. We might as well die with him.'

When Jesus finally got there, he found Lazarus already four days dead. Bethany was near Jerusalem, only a couple of miles away, and many of the Jews were visiting Martha and Mary, sympathizing with them over their brother. Martha heard Jesus was coming and went out to meet him. Mary remained in the house.

Martha said, 'Master, if you'd been here, my brother wouldn't have died. Even now, I know that whatever you ask God he will give you.'

Jesus said, 'Your brother will be raised up.'

Martha replied, 'I know that he will be raised up in the resurrection at the end of time.'

'You don't have to wait for the End. I am, right now, Resurrection and Life. The one who believes in me, even though he or she dies, will live. And everyone who lives believing in me does not ultimately die at all. Do you believe this?'

'Yes, Master. All along I have believed that you are the Messiah, the Son of God who comes into the world.'

After saying this, she went to her sister Mary and whispered in her ear, 'The Teacher is here and is asking for you.'

The moment she heard that, she jumped up and ran out to him. Jesus had not yet entered the town but was still at the place where Martha had met him. When her sympathizing Jewish friends saw Mary run off, they followed her, thinking she was on her way to the tomb to weep there. Mary came to where Jesus was waiting and fell at his feet, saying, 'Master, if only you had been here, my brother would not have died.'

When Jesus saw her sobbing and the Jews with her sobbing, a deep anger welled up within him. He said, 'Where did you put him?'

'Master, come and see,' they said. Now Jesus wept.

The Jews said, 'Look how deeply he loved him.'

Others among them said, 'Well, if he loved him so much, why didn't he do something to keep him from dying? After all, he opened the eyes of a blind man.'

Then Jesus, the anger again welling up within him, arrived at the tomb. It was a simple cave in the hillside with a slab of stone laid against it. Jesus said, 'Remove the stone.'

The sister of the dead man, Martha, said, 'Master, by this time there's a stench. He's been dead four days!'

Jesus looked her in the eye. 'Didn't I tell you that if you believed, you would see the glory of God?'

Then, to the others, 'Go ahead, take away the stone.'

They removed the stone. Jesus raised his eyes to heaven

and prayed, 'Father, I'm grateful that you have listened to me. I know you always do listen, but on account of this crowd standing here I've spoken so that they might believe that you sent me.'

Then he shouted, 'Lazarus, come out!' And he came out, a cadaver, wrapped from head to toe, and with a kerchief over his face.

Jesus told them, 'Unwrap him and let him loose.'

Discussion Starters

1. Why was the village in this story called 'the town of Mary and Martha' (v.1)?

---

2. Why did Jesus weep?

---

3. How does Martha react in this situation compared to the time when Jesus visits her home in Luke 10:38–42? What is the difference in Mary's reaction?

4. What is meant by: 'Are there not twelve hours of daylight? Anyone who walks in the daytime will not stumble, for they see by this world's light. It is when a person walks at night that they stumble, for they have no light' (vv.9–10)?

_____

_____

_____

_____

_____

5. Jesus says, 'Unwrap him and let him loose' (v.44). Are you aware of any areas in your life where you feel restricted or trapped in some way? Share your thoughts with the group if you feel able to.

_____

_____

_____

_____

_____

6. Lazarus heard Jesus say, 'Lazarus, come out!' (v.43)
How do you respond when God calls you to do something?

_____

_____

_____

_____

_____

7. Lazarus could not unbind himself, he needed help.
How can we help each other walk into greater freedom?

_____

_____

_____

_____

8. Do you believe that God can raise people from the dead today?

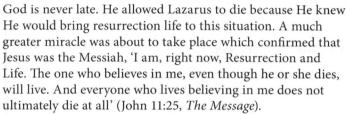

Final Thoughts

God is never late. He allowed Lazarus to die because He knew
He would bring resurrection life to this situation. A much
greater miracle was about to take place which confirmed that
Jesus was the Messiah, 'I am, right now, Resurrection and
Life. The one who believes in me, even though he or she dies,
will live. And everyone who lives believing in me does not
ultimately die at all' (John 11:25, *The Message*).

We too are required to wait and waiting requires trust
and obedience. It is not a passive process, but an active one.
It involves seeking God, praying, listening and meditating
on His Word. Much of the spiritual life involves waiting and
during the waiting important training takes place, like a form
of boot camp. In the waiting we are changed – made ready
for the next stage of the journey. The process reminds me of
a relay race in which a runner waits with expectancy inside
the box ready to receive the baton and sprint the next leg of
the race. The runner is not sitting around relaxing in the relay
box, but is alert and ready to run the race of their life as soon
as they are handed the baton. We too must wait for God's
timing, because if we run on ahead without God, we are at
risk of 'running' in our own strength and are likely to burn
out or collapse.

Waiting builds character and can release us from unhelpful
and sinful patterns of behaviour. It also teaches us to rely on
God and increases our stability. In fact, those who wait for God
renew their strength, they 'soar on wings like eagles' rising above
their problems (Isa. 40:31).

But sometimes God allows a situation to go from bad to
worse because He is planning to do something more powerful

and transformative in our lives – He has a purpose that will bring even more glory to God.

Closing Prayer

Lord, give us Your peace in the waiting and help us to look to You to sustain us. Teach us, transform us and renew us so that we can soar on eagle's wings above our problems. And, as we wait, help us to lean against You and to trust in Your perfect timing. Amen.

Further Reflection

Busy or Listening? – Imaginative Meditation

Take your time to pause in between the questions and sentences below, or use my recording of 'Busy or Listening?'. This imaginative meditation voiced over music is available from my website: **www.lizbabbs.com**

I wonder what your reaction would be, if Jesus came to visit your home?

Imagine Jesus knocking on your door now.

What would be your immediate reaction?

Would you rush round clearing up? Or would you invite Him in immediately?

Which part of the house would you show Him in to?

What would your first words to Him be?

Would you make Him a drink, or cook Him a meal, or just sit and chat?

Now as I read you the story of Mary and Martha, imagine yourself stepping inside their house, just as Jesus did ...

(Luke 10:38-42, TNIV)

As Jesus and his disciples were on their way, he came to a village where a woman named Martha opened her home to him. She had a sister called Mary, who sat at the Lord's feet listening to what he said. But Martha was distracted by all the preparations that had to be made. She came to him and asked, 'Lord, don't you care that my sister has left me to do the work for myself? Tell her to help me!'

'Martha, Martha,' the Lord answered, 'you are worried and upset about many things, but only one thing is needed. Mary has chosen what is better, and it will not be taken away from her.'

As you reflect on this scripture, read from another translation, I'd like you to imagine that you are Mary sitting at the feet of Jesus enjoying His company. Visualise yourself sitting next to Him now.

What are you sitting on. Or are you kneeling?

Where is Jesus sitting?

Is He sitting on your right or left?

What is He wearing?

What is He saying to you?

Is there anything you'd like to ask Him?

Is there anything you would you like to say to Martha?

How does your time with Jesus end?

(Luke 10:38-42, *The Message*)

As they continued their travel, Jesus entered a village. A woman by the name of Martha welcomed him and made him feel quite at home. She had a sister, Mary, who sat before the Master, hanging on every word he said. But Martha was pulled away by all she

had to do in the kitchen. Later, she stepped in, interrupting them. 'Master, don't you care that my sister has abandoned the kitchen to me? Tell her to lend me a hand.'

The Master said, 'Martha, dear Martha, you're fussing far too much and getting yourself worked up over nothing. One thing only is essential, and Mary has chosen it, ... and [it] won't be taken from her.'

Named by Jesus

John 20:1-18

Icebreaker

Discuss with others or consider independently the different ways in which people use your Christian name. For example, I am known as Elizabeth by my mother, Lizzy by my nieces, nephews and close friends, but I'm called Liz by everyone else. When I started writing my first book *Can God Help ME?* (Authentic Media: 2003), I used my full name Elizabeth because I discovered it meant 'consecrated to God,' and I wanted my first book to be dedicated to God.

How do others use *your* name?

Opening prayer

Lord, thank You that You have called us by name and we are completely Yours, loved and adored. Thank You that Your care is everlasting. You know us intimately – every hair on our head is numbered by You. Help us to gain a greater understanding of what it means to be known by You and show us how much we mean to You. Amen.

Bible Passages

Isaiah 49:16 (NLT)
See, I have written your name on the palms of my hands.

Isaiah 43:1-2 (NLT)
I have called you by name; you are mine.
When you go through deep waters,
I will be with you.
When you go through rivers of difficulty,
you will not drown.

Deuteronomy 32:10
In a desert land he found him,
in a barren and howling waste.
He shielded him and cared for him;
he guarded him as the apple of his eye.

Luke 10:20
However, do not rejoice that the spirits submit to you,

but rejoice that your names are written in heaven.

Psalm 148:13
Let them praise the name of the LORD,
for his name alone is exalted;
his splendor is above the earth and the heavens.

Psalm 68:11 (NIV, 2011)
The Lord announces the word, and the women who
proclaim it are a mighty throng.

Eye Opener

When I was a toddler, my grandad had an extension, a covered
walkway, added to the side of his house. When cement was
being laid down to support the framework of the new walkway,
he wrote my name 'Liz' in the wet cement. I loved that my
name was written in the grounds of his house and always
rushed to see it when visiting them. I was so sad when, aged
eight, we moved over a hundred miles away. Not only did
I miss my grandparents terribly, but I would no longer see
my name in cement. Thirty years later when their house was
demolished, I was devastated – so many of my childhood
memories were wrapped up in that house. My name was
written into its foundations, but now it was gone for ever.
Our names, because of Jesus, are written into something that
cannot be destroyed; they are 'written in heaven' (Luke 10:20).

Setting the Scene

The resurrection is pivotal to our faith, because without it,
Christianity is just another religion. To quote Paul, 'And if
Christ has not been raised, our preaching is useless and so
is your faith' (1 Cor. 15:14). Jesus chose to make His first
resurrection appearance to a woman called Mary Magdalene.
Mary Magdalene was present at many key events including
the crucifixion. She, along with Mary, mother of Jesus, even
saw where Jesus was laid after the crucifixion (Mark 15:47).
The Gospel of Mark tells us that this is the Mary from whom
Jesus had 'cast out seven demons' (Mark 16:9).

It's incredible to think that Jesus' first appearance as the risen Saviour was at the tomb with Mary Magdalene and she thought He was a gardener! It's rather like mistaking the Queen for a shop assistant! For Jesus to appear to a woman would have been shocking enough in that culture, but to appear to a woman from whom He had cast out demons was incredible. But then, Jesus loved women and often broke with convention by ministering to the marginalised. Mary must have been overwhelmed to see Jesus again. Imagine the significance of that moment when she heard Jesus call her name.

Session Focus

Relax, close your eyes and come and meet Jesus at the garden tomb with Mary. As you listen to this passage of Scripture read to you several times, see if any words or sentences stand out or become highlighted in some way. At the end of the readings, spend a couple of minutes in silence asking God to show you what He might be saying to you through any words, thoughts or images that drop into your mind. Then discuss your thoughts with your group or take time to record them for your own personal reflection.

The Empty Tomb (John 20:1-10)

Early on the first day of the week, while it was still dark, Mary Magdalene went to the tomb and saw that the stone had been removed from the entrance. So she came running to Simon Peter and the other disciple, the one Jesus loved, and said, 'They have taken the Lord out of the tomb, and we don't know where they have put him!'

So Peter and the other disciple started for the tomb. Both were running, but the other disciple outran Peter and reached the tomb first. He bent over and looked in at the strips of linen lying there but did not go in. Then Simon Peter, who was behind him, arrived and went into the tomb. He saw the strips of linen lying there, as well as the burial cloth that had been around Jesus' head. The cloth was folded up by itself, separate from the linen. Finally the other disciple, who had reached the tomb first, also went inside. He saw and believed. (They still did not understand from Scripture that Jesus had to rise from the dead.)

Jesus Appears to Mary Magdalene (John 20:10-18)

Then the disciples went back to their homes, but Mary stood outside the tomb crying. As she wept, she bent over to look into the tomb and saw two angels in white, seated where Jesus' body had been, one at the head and the other at the foot.

They asked her, 'Woman, why are you crying?'

'They have taken my Lord away,' she said, 'and I don't know where they have put him.' At this, she turned around and saw Jesus standing there, but she did not realise that it was Jesus.

'Woman,' he said, 'why are you crying? Who is it you are looking for?'

Thinking he was the gardener, she said, 'Sir, if you have carried him away, tell me where you have put him, and I will get him.'

Jesus said to her, 'Mary.' She turned toward him and cried out in Aramaic, 'Rabboni!' (which means Teacher).

Jesus said, 'Do not hold on to me, for I have not yet returned to the Father. Go instead to my brothers and tell them, "I am returning to my Father and your Father, to my God and your God."'

Mary Magdalene went to the disciples with the news: 'I have seen the Lord!' And she told them that he had said these things to her.

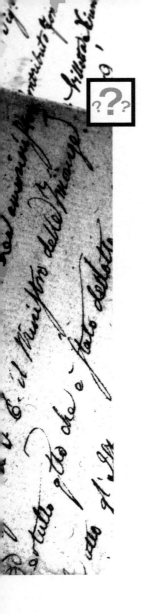

Discussion Starters

1. Why didn't Mary recognise Jesus at first?

2. Why wasn't Mary shocked to see angels there? What part do angels play in this passage?

3. Who was the disciple 'Jesus loved' (v.2) and why was he referred to in this way?

4. Can you picture Jesus' facial expression as He said, 'Mary' (v.16)? If so, describe it.

5. What might Mary's reaction have been to hearing her name spoken by Jesus?

_____

_____

_____

_____

_____

6. There are many ways that Mary could have responded to Jesus. Why do you think she called him 'Rabboni' meaning teacher (v.16)?

_____

_____

_____

_____

_____

7. Why did Jesus say to her: 'Woman ... why are you crying? Who is it you are looking for' (v.15)?

_____

_____

_____

_____

_____

8. Why did Jesus not want Mary to hold on to Him?

_____

_____

_____

_____

_____

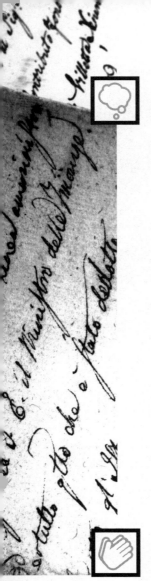

Final Thoughts

When I was Captain and Centre Forward for the school hockey team, those on my team used to shout, 'Run, Babbsy, run.' I know they were only cheering me on to score a goal, but somehow being called Babbsy depersonalised me. I felt like a number rather than a human being, like the number '9' I was wearing on my back.

Someone once called me Babbsy in church too and I was cross. I still felt the sting of being called Babbsy at school. But again, the person did not mean to offend me and was probably just using my surname affectionately.

Jesus could have said much at that first resurrection appearance in the garden, but He chose to say just one word, 'Mary.' His greeting was personal and intimate, revealing His identity and restoring Mary's hope and joy.

Our names are important to us. When someone uses my name it means they know me in some way. They are talking *to* me rather than at me. Our names are important to God too; we are His masterpiece and all great masterpieces bear the artist's signature (Eph. 2:10). Mary mattered so much to Jesus that He made her His first priority. She must have burst with joy when she realised that it was Jesus calling her. Jesus meant everything to Mary, so no wonder she wanted to hold on to Him one last time. Jesus had rescued her from captivity and released her into the fullness of His love, and those who have been forgiven much love much.

Closing Prayer

Lord Jesus, thank You that through Your death and resurrection we belong to You. Help us to understand the fullness of that priceless inheritance You died to give us. Amen.

Further Reflection

Called by Name - Imaginative Meditation

Take your time to pause in between the questions and sentences below, or use my recording of 'Called by Name'. This imaginative meditation voiced over music is available from my website: **www.lizbabbs.com**

I'd like to invite you to step into the Bible story where Mary Magdalene meets Jesus at the tomb after the resurrection.

Imagine yourself walking into the scene now and meeting Jesus at the tomb.

What you can see?

Can you smell anything?

Or hear anything?

I wonder how you're feeling?

Imagine Jesus tenderly calling your name ....
(insert your name here).

And what is your response?

Do you recognise Jesus? And if so, what might you say to Him?

And is He saying anything to you?

And now just relax and enjoy Jesus' company.

Faith and Jesus
Matthew 14:22-36

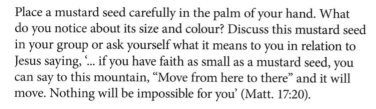

Icebreaker

Place a mustard seed carefully in the palm of your hand. What do you notice about its size and colour? Discuss this mustard seed in your group or ask yourself what it means to you in relation to Jesus saying, '... if you have faith as small as a mustard seed, you can say to this mountain, "Move from here to there" and it will move. Nothing will be impossible for you' (Matt. 17:20).

Opening Prayer

Lord, help us to plant our tiny mustard seed of faith in You, knowing that in You it will multiply. And Lord, I pray that You would expand our vision and knowledge so that we too would have the kind of faith that moves mountains and walks on water. Amen.

Bible Readings

Deuteronomy 31:6
Be strong and courageous. Do not be afraid or terrified because of them, for the LORD your God goes with you; he will never leave you nor forsake you.

Isaiah 41:10
So do not fear, for I am with you;
do not be dismayed, for I am your God.
I will strengthen you and help you;
I will uphold you with my righteous right hand.

Psalm 32:8
I will instruct you and teach you in the way you should go;
I will counsel you and watch over you.

John 14:27 (Amp)
Peace I leave with you; My [own] peace I now give *and* bequeath to you. Not as the world gives do I give to you. Do not let your hearts be troubled, neither let them be afraid. [Stop allowing yourselves to be agitated and disturbed; and do not permit yourselves to be fearful and intimidated and cowardly and unsettled.]

Hebrews 11:6

And without faith it is impossible to please God, because anyone who comes to him must believe that he exists and that he rewards those who earnestly seek him.

Eye Opener

Have you ever had a crisis of confidence? I have, and it was the last time I performed my one-woman show, which showcases my work as a writer and performer. I've performed that show many times, but it had been nearly a year since the last performance and I felt unsettled and agitated. I prayed beforehand, but when I arrived and saw how large and informal the venue was, I started to panic. Instead of looking to Jesus for strength, I began to sink into worry, concerned as to whether I'd even survive the evening! That's what happens when you give in to fear. On that occasion, I grew increasingly hot and uncomfortable so I went outside for some fresh air to calm myself down, and then texted a few friends asking them to pray.

If only I had trusted God, because just ten minutes later a friend from church walked into the venue. She had come to support me. Wow! God had provided one of my friends at a vital time when I thought I was going under. Although I was almost engulfed by the wave of worry, I didn't drown and the audience couldn't have been more appreciative. It turned out to be a great evening!

I, like Peter, called by Jesus to walk on water, trusted God, but not quite fully enough. It's amazing to think that Jesus called Peter His 'rock' (Matt. 16:18) and on that 'rock' He would build the future of the Church!

Setting the Scene

After feeding the 5,000, Jesus sends His disciples ahead of Him in a boat across the Sea of Galilee while He goes up a mountain to spend time with His Father in prayer. Some hours later, during the night, the disciples encounter a violent storm about three miles from the shore. Try picturing it.

The disciples, who are very experienced fishermen, have been rowing for hours against the wind and are exhausted. Then Jesus, out of nowhere, walks to them on the water. No wonder they were shocked and started screaming, they thought they were seeing a ghost! So Jesus reassures them and tells them it's Him, saying in effect, 'Don't worry! I am Jesus. Don't be afraid.'

Walking on water is not normal human behaviour and so I bet they were very relieved to know it was Him. But Jesus demonstrates that water-walking isn't just for the Messiah, but for anyone Jesus calls, like Peter. It is only when Peter begins to look down at the size of the waves, taking his focus off Jesus, that he begins to sink.

Session Focus

Relax, close your eyes and come on a journey to meet Peter and the disciples as they encounter the risen Christ. As you listen to this passage of Scripture read to you several times, see if any words or sentences stand out or become highlighted in some way. At the end of the readings, spend a couple of minutes in silence asking God to show you what He might be saying to you through any words, thoughts or images that drop into your mind. Then discuss your thoughts with your group or take time to record them for your own personal reflection.

Jesus Walks on the Water (Matthew 14:22-36)

Immediately Jesus made the disciples get into the boat and go on ahead of him to the other side, while he dismissed the crowd. After he had dismissed them, he went up on a mountainside by himself to pray. When evening came, he was there alone, but the boat was already a considerable distance from land, buffeted by the waves because the wind was against it.

During the fourth watch of the night Jesus went out to them, walking on the lake. When the disciples saw him walking on the lake, they were terrified. 'It's a ghost,' they said, and cried out in fear.

But Jesus immediately said to them: 'Take courage! It is I.

Don't be afraid.'

'Lord, if it's you,' Peter replied, 'tell me to come to you on the water.'

'Come,' he said.

Then Peter got down out of the boat, walked on the water and came toward Jesus. But when he saw the wind, he was afraid and, beginning to sink, cried out, 'Lord, save me!'

Immediately Jesus reached out his hand and caught him. 'You of little faith,' he said, 'why did you doubt?'

And when they climbed into the boat, the wind died down. Then those who were in the boat worshiped him, saying, 'Truly you are the Son of God.'

When they had crossed over, they landed at Gennesaret. And when the men of that place recognised Jesus, they sent word to all the surrounding country. People brought all their sick to him and begged him to let the sick just touch the edge of his cloak, and all who touched him were healed.

Discussion Starters

1. How would you describe faith? And how does faith grow?

_____

_____

_____

_____

_____

2. Seeking solitude was a priority for Jesus. He often went across a lake or up a mountain to pray. How do you make time for solitude? Why is solitude important?

_____

_____

_____

_____

_____

3. Why did Jesus call Peter out of the boat and not any of the other disciples?

_____

_____

_____

_____

_____

4. 'And now these three remain: faith, hope and love. But the greatest of these is love' (1 Cor. 13:13). Why is love more important than faith and hope?

_____

_____

_____

_____

_____

5. Why did Peter say, 'Lord, if it's you, tell me to come to you on the water'(v.28)?

_____

_____

_____

_____

_____

6. Why did Peter start to sink? What makes you 'look down at the water'?

_____

_____

_____

_____

_____

7. Are there ways you could take more risks in your faith?

_____

_____

_____

_____

8. Prayers don't have to be long to be effective. Peter utters possibly one of the shortest prayers in the Bible, 'Lord, save me!' (v.30). Share with the group some of the short prayers you pray when you find yourself in a difficult situation.

_____

_____

_____

_____

Final Thoughts

Faith is central to the Christian life. The key to faith, as Paul states, is to know the one in whom you are trusting (see Phil. 3:10). It is not self-confidence, but God-confidence. It's about planting our tiny mustard seed of faith in a large God and expecting results.

Hebrews tells us that, '... without faith it is impossible to please God, because anyone who comes to him must believe that he exists ...' (Heb. 11:6). Faith is about having confidence and trust in the person we are believing in. The Bible gives this description of faith: 'Now faith is being sure of what we hope for and certain of what we do not see' (Heb. 11:1). So, no wonder it feels like we're walking a tightrope at times.

Scripture also tells us that faith is a gift from God: 'For it is by grace you have been saved, through faith – and this not from yourselves, it is the gift of God ...' (Eph. 2:8). With this gift of faith we can speak to mountains and see miracles happen.

Faith requires us to take risks. But then living is a risk. Every time we cross the road, get into our cars or board a plane etc, we risk accidents, but then, accidents can happen at home too. Peter walking on the water is a picture of us being willing to step out fully into God's plan for our life. Unfortunately many of us are unwilling to take the risk because we prefer to stay in our comfort zones. But Jesus' life was far from comfortable: He embraced risk wherever He travelled. Faith, like a rollercoaster, can take us on quite a ride, and so if we don't hold on tightly to God we'll struggle to survive, especially when we go upside down looping the loop!

In order to overcome our circumstances, it is also essential we know the power and authority we possess in God so that we can stand firm against the devil who seeks to cause chaos by sowing doubt and fear in our minds. But God has given us spiritual riot gear to deal with the devil, including a shield of faith (Eph. 6:16) to extinguish the devil's missiles. Plus we have the sword of the Spirit (Eph. 6:17), so, like Jesus in the desert, we can brandish our swords proclaiming, 'It is written ...' (Matt. 4:4,7,10). In God we have the authority to defeat the devil, provided we fix our eyes on God and not our circumstances. Like David, when he killed Goliath using a simple sling and stone, we need to say to ourselves, 'With God, how can I miss!'

Closing Prayer

Thank You, Lord, that You never let go of us, even when we lose trust in You and begin to doubt in Your promises. Help us to fully realise that no matter what we go through You will be there for us. Help us, like Peter, to have the faith to know that through us You can do even greater things, more than we ever dreamed or imagined. Amen.

Further Reflection

Walk on Water – Imaginative Meditation

Take your time to pause in between the questions and sentences below, or use my recording of 'Walk on Water'. This imaginative meditation voiced over music is available from my website: **www.lizbabbs.com**

I'd like to invite you to step into the Bible story where Jesus walks on the water.

Imagine that Jesus is inviting you now to get out of the boat and to walk to Him on the water. Are you willing to take the risk?

Imagine yourself stepping out on to the water now ...

How does it feel?

What can you see?

What can you hear?

What are people back in the boat saying?

How far away from Jesus are you?

What are you saying to Jesus?

And what is Jesus saying to you?

How far away are you from Jesus now?

And when you finally meet with Jesus, what does He say and do?

And what's your response?

And how does your encounter with Jesus end?

Obedience and Jesus
John 21:1-14

Icebreaker

Did you ever play Chinese Whispers as a child? Try it now with your group. One of you whispers a sentence of around five to ten words about something that happened today. The person sitting next to you then whispers this sentence to the person next to them ... and so on around the group. When the last person has heard the message, they then repeat it aloud to the group to see if it's the same message as at the beginning. Alternatively, if you are studying this book independently, try turning the volume off on your TV or computer for a few minutes. How much of the programme can you understand?

Opening Prayer

Lord, we long to hear You and, like Samuel, to say 'Speak, for your servant is listening' (1 Sam. 3:10). Quieten our bodies, still our minds and help us to surrender all our worries and concerns to You, knowing that Your yoke is easy and Your burden light. Amen.

Bible Readings

Job 33:14 (NLT)
For God speaks again and again,
though people do not recognize it.

Isaiah 65:24
Before they call I will answer;
while they are still speaking I will hear.

1 Peter 1:14
As obedient children, do not conform to the evil desires you had when you lived in ignorance.

Romans 10:17 (NASB)
So faith *comes* from hearing, and hearing by the word of Christ.

1 Kings 19:12
After the earthquake came a fire, but the LORD was not in the fire. And after the fire came a gentle whisper.

STUDY | **SIX**

Eye Opener

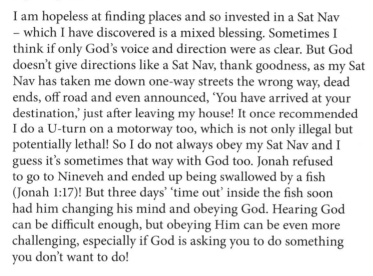

I am hopeless at finding places and so invested in a Sat Nav – which I have discovered is a mixed blessing. Sometimes I think if only God's voice and direction were as clear. But God doesn't give directions like a Sat Nav, thank goodness, as my Sat Nav has taken me down one-way streets the wrong way, dead ends, off road and even announced, 'You have arrived at your destination,' just after leaving my house! It once recommended I do a U-turn on a motorway too, which is not only illegal but potentially lethal! So I do not always obey my Sat Nav and I guess it's sometimes that way with God too. Jonah refused to go to Nineveh and ended up being swallowed by a fish (Jonah 1:17)! But three days' 'time out' inside the fish soon had him changing his mind and obeying God. Hearing God can be difficult enough, but obeying Him can be even more challenging, especially if God is asking you to do something you don't want to do!

Setting the Scene

Chapter 21 of John's Gospel opens with a miraculous catch of fish where Jesus begins to direct, affirm and encourage His team of disciples. And they soon realise that their enormous catch of fish is only possible under Jesus' direction and anointing. This is Jesus' third appearance to His disciples since the resurrection, making sure they understood that He was risen from the dead. It is also a reminder of the calling of the first disciples, where Jesus told them, 'From now on you'll be fishing for people' (Luke 5:10, NLT).

The disciples were not only learning how to 'Put out into deep water, and let down [their] nets for a catch' (Luke 5:4), but also how to fish on the right side of the boat – the side Jesus directed them to fish on. Peter thinks it's a waste of time and tells Jesus so, but then obeys, 'But because you say so, I will let down the nets' (Luke 5:5). The resulting catch is so large that their nets begin to break. And then Jesus cooks them breakfast – a barbeque on the beach!

Session Focus

Relax, close your eyes and come on a journey with Peter and the disciples as they meet Jesus after the resurrection. As you listen to this passage of Scripture read to you several times, see if any words or sentences stand out or become highlighted in some way. At the end of the readings, spend a couple of minutes in silence asking God to show you what He might be saying to you through any words, thoughts or images that drop into your mind. Then discuss your thoughts with your group or take time to record them for your own personal reflection.

Jesus and the Miraculous Catch of Fish (John 21:1-14)

Afterward Jesus appeared again to his disciples, by the Sea of Tiberias. It happened this way: Simon Peter, Thomas (also known as Didymus), Nathanael from Cana in Galilee, the sons of Zebedee, and two other disciples were together. 'I'm going out to fish,' Simon Peter told them, and they said, 'We'll go with you.' So they went out and got into the boat, but that night they caught nothing.

Early in the morning, Jesus stood on the shore, but the disciples did not realise that it was Jesus.

He called out to them, 'Friends, haven't you any fish?'

'No,' they answered.

He said, 'Throw your net on the right side of the boat and you will find some.' When they did, they were unable to haul the net in because of the large number of fish.

Then the disciple whom Jesus loved said to Peter, 'It is the Lord!' As soon as Simon Peter heard him say, 'It is the Lord,' he wrapped his outer garment around him (for he had taken it off) and jumped into the water. The other disciples followed in the boat, towing the net full of fish, for they were not far from shore, about a hundred yards. When they landed, they saw a fire of burning coals there with fish on it, and some bread.

Jesus said to them, 'Bring some of the fish you have just caught.'

Simon Peter climbed aboard and dragged the net ashore.

It was full of large fish, 153, but even with so many the net was not torn. Jesus said to them, 'Come and have breakfast.' None of the disciples dared ask him, 'Who are you?' They knew it was the Lord. Jesus came, took the bread and gave it to them, and did the same with the fish. This was now the third time Jesus appeared to his disciples after he was raised from the dead.

Discussion Starters

1. The disciples hadn't caught any fish. Were they doing anything wrong?

_____

_____

_____

_____

_____

2. Why did Peter wrap something around himself and jump into the water once he knew it was Jesus?

_____

_____

_____

_____

_____

3. How did the disciples know it was Jesus?

_____

_____

_____

_____

_____

4. How can we tell whether it is God speaking to us or just our imagination?

_____

_____

_____

_____

_____

5. How do you think you hear God?

_____

_____

_____

_____

_____

6. Why do some people say they can't hear God?

_____

_____

_____

_____

_____

7. Hearing God is just the beginning. How important is obedience?

_____

_____

_____

_____

_____

8. Why do you think Jesus made so many resurrection appearances before He ascended into heaven?

_____

_____

_____

_____

Final Thoughts

Chapter 21 of John's Gospel was added to an already finished Gospel to demonstrate the reality of the resurrection which is central to Christianity. Without it, it could have been said that Christ's appearances were simply visions or the disciples' imaginations working overtime! However, this chapter clearly demonstrates that Jesus was not a ghost or apparition. He was a real person who'd conquered death and was now directing a fishing trip, eating breakfast with His disciples and breaking bread.

The disciples were lost without Jesus and their fishing trip was only successful when He appeared to them and gave them instructions on where to fish. Jesus was teaching the disciples not only about the importance of listening to Him, but also of being obedient to His direction so they could be more fruitful. The miraculous catch of fish is a symbolic reference to the disciples being fishers of people, and is a call to mission.

Shortly after this, the risen Christ takes the time to train Peter to listen and obey Him. He was preparing him to be a great shepherd to God's sheep. Jesus asks Peter three times if he loves Him, to give him three opportunities to declare his love for Him, because he had previously denied Jesus three times. As Peter confirms his love for Jesus, he is reinstated and called to pastoral mission, 'Feed my sheep,' Jesus says (John 21:17). Peter's fall did not invalidate his call.

It makes an interesting study to read all Jesus' resurrection appearances in the Gospels, because in each one of them, He is not immediately recognised. It takes a familiar word or gesture for the disciples to recognise Him; we have seen this in our studies on the Road to Emmaus, with Mary at the tomb, and in this passage. Jesus is somehow different – transformed – and in the transformation continues to transform the lives of others, including ourselves today.

Closing Prayer

Lord, lead us into a place of deeper intimacy with You. Calm our doubts and make clear our life's direction. Ignite our passion so that we might be obedient to Your call upon our lives. Amen.

Further Reflection

Coffee with Jesus – Imaginative Meditation

Take your time to pause in between the questions and sentences below, or use my recording of 'Coffee with Jesus'. This imaginative meditation voiced over music is available from my website: **www.lizbabbs.com**

I'd like you to imagine you're meeting Jesus for a coffee.

Where are you?

What are you drinking?

What are you saying to Jesus?

And is Jesus saying anything to you?

Is there anything you'd like to discuss with Jesus?

Do you have any specific tasks you need to complete today?

And how does Jesus respond to these?

And is there something specific that Jesus is asking you to do?

And what's your response?

And now just relax and enjoy Jesus' company.

Leader's Notes

General Notes on Leading the Studies

The aim of the six studies in this book is to take people on a journey deeper into God as they meet well-known characters from the Bible and observe how their lives have been transformed by the presence of Jesus. The approach I've taken is both interactive and reflective, encouraging individuals to understand Scripture from the inside out.

I have written each Session Focus section in the studies so that it can be approached reflectively. This allows individuals and members of the group to step inside the passage of Scripture and encourages a heart response, not just a head one. It also gives the group the opportunity to engage with the passage experientially before more traditional Bible discussion questions might be used afterwards. Questions may well arise out of this time of reflection too, but this approach initiates a response from group members, which is very valuable in the learning process.

At the beginning of each Session Focus I have written a short introduction:

Relax, close your eyes and come on a journey ... As you listen to this passage of Scripture read to you several times, see if any words or sentences stand out or become highlighted in some way. At the end of the readings, spend a couple of minutes in silence asking God to show you what He might be saying to you through any words, thoughts or images that drop into your mind. Then discuss your thoughts with your group or take time to record them for your own personal reflection.

How to Lead the Session Focus Reflectively

Here are some ideas to help you as you lead these sections of the book:

1. At the beginning of each Session Focus you could pray, 'Lord, we pray that You would speak to us through Your Word and like Samuel we pray, "Speak, for your servant is listening."'

2. It is best if group members don't look up the passage for the first reading. Encourage them to relax, put their books and pens down and close their eyes as you read the passage slowly to them. Then ask them to see if any words, thoughts, images or sentences stand out from the passage (as though they were highlighted by a marker pen).

3. At the end of the first reading give them a few minutes to reflect in silence and to ask God to show them how He might be speaking to them through their highlighted word or words.

4. Then read the passage through slowly again, or use a Bible audio recording such as *The Bible Experience* (Zondervan). If individuals want to follow the passage this time, they can, but it is not necessary. (They are welcome to look anything up at the end of this second reading.)

5. Having read the passage aloud twice to the group, give them a few minutes, again to reflect on their personal highlighted word and what God might be saying to them.

6. Then ask them to share their thoughts, highlighted words or questions with the group.

- To encourage this personal sharing, explain that sharing thoughts and ideas with the group can help those who feel they have not received anything specific as the passage is read. It is also important that there is no pressure to share or to share more personally than a person might wish.

- If you are short of time, you could just read the passage once instead of twice, especially if it is a much longer passage, eg John 11:1–44 in Study Three.

Study One: Walking with Jesus

Icebreaker
Hand out scrap paper and pens. Do not allow group members to spend longer than five minutes creating their line drawing because otherwise they run the danger of over-processing. Then encourage them to share their drawings if they feel comfortable doing so.

Bible Readings
These are centred on walking with God, whereas the main Bible passage for the session 'On the Road to Emmaus' is focused on God walking with the disciples and us.

Session Focus – Luke 24:13-35
It's interesting to note here that Jesus doesn't just appear to His top ten disciples, the first league, or A-list, but also to D-list folk like Cleopas and an unknown disciple. Jesus wanted to know what was on their hearts even though He already knew!

Final Thoughts
We also need the 'eyes of our hearts' open so that we can see Jesus and His footprints across our lives. And we need to allow Him to break bread with us so that we can enter into a deeper communion with Him.

Further Reflection
The most effective way to lead this imaginative meditation is to use the 'The Emmaus Road' audio download or CD available from my website: **www.lizbabbs.com**

This track could also be used in between sessions as a personal meditation by individuals in the group.

Study Two: Known by Jesus

Bible Readings
These focus on the importance of being known and accepted by Jesus.

Discussion Starters
Question 3 – Group members don't have to share their 1–10 scale on how accepted they feel by God, unless they are comfortable doing so. Remind them also that feelings can often be an unreliable indicator.

Further Reflection
The most effective way to lead this imaginative meditation is to use the 'The Woman at the Well' audio download or CD available from my website: **www.lizbabbs.com**

This track could also be used in between sessions as a personal meditation by individuals in the group.

Study Three: Waiting for Jesus

Icebreaker

Delay serving drinks to your group until *after* you've started the study. Ask the group what their reaction was to not being served a drink as soon as they arrive. How did they feel not receiving what they had anticipated? Alternatively, if you are studying this book independently, delay one of your refreshment breaks by an hour and note your reaction.

Session Focus –John 11:1–44

I've used *The Message* translation here instead of the NIV. But you could use a different translation the second time you read it, if you prefer.

Further Reflection

The most effective way to lead this imaginative meditation is to use the 'Busy or Listening?' audio download or CD available from my website: **www.lizbabbs.com**

This track could also be used in between sessions as a personal meditation by individuals in the group.

Study Four: Named by Jesus

Further Reflection

The most effective way to lead this imaginative meditation is to use the 'Called by Name' audio download or CD available from my website: **www.lizbabbs.com**

This track could also be used in between sessions as a personal meditation by individuals in the group.

Study Five: Faith and Jesus

Icebreaker
Mustard cress seeds work well for this icebreaker. Group members can even plant their seed after the session and watch it grow across the remaining weeks of Lent.

Further Reflection
The most effective way to lead this imaginative meditation is to use the 'Walk on Water' audio download or CD available from my website: **www.lizbabbs.com**

This track could also be used in between sessions as a personal meditation by individuals in the group.

Study Six: Obedience and Jesus

Icebreaker
The focus here is on the importance of hearing accurately.

Bible Readings
The focus of these readings is on hearing and obeying God.

Session Focus – John 21:1-14
It would be helpful if, prior to the study, you read Luke 5:1–11 where Jesus calls the first disciples, as this passage links with John 21:1–14.

Further Reflection
The most effective way to lead this imaginative meditation is to use the 'Coffee with Jesus' audio download or CD available from my website: **www.lizbabbs.com**

This track could also be used in between sessions as a personal meditation by individuals in the group.

To find out more about the meditative technique see Liz Babbs' website: http://www.lizbabbs.com/shop/into-gods-presence

National Distributors

UK: (and countries not listed below)

CWR, Waverley Abbey House, Waverley Lane, Farnham, Surrey GU9 8EP.
Tel: (01252) 784700 Outside UK (44) 1252 784700 Email: mail@cwr.org.uk

AUSTRALIA: KI Entertainment, Unit 21 317-321 Woodpark Road, Smithfield, New South Wales 2164.
Tel: 1 800 850 777 Fax: 02 9604 3699 Email: sales@kientertainment.com.au

CANADA: David C Cook Distribution Canada, PO Box 98, 55 Woodslee Avenue, Paris, Ontario N3L 3E5.
Tel: 1800 263 2664 Email: sandi.swanson@davidccook.ca

GHANA: Challenge Enterprises of Ghana, PO Box 5723, Accra.
Tel: (021) 222437/223249 Fax: (021) 226227 Email: ceg@africaonline.com.gh

HONG KONG: Cross Communications Ltd, 1/F, 562A Nathan Road, Kowloon.
Tel: 2780 1188 Fax: 2770 6229 Email: cross@crosshk.com

INDIA: Crystal Communications, 10-3-18/4/1, East Marredpalli, Secunderabad – 500026,
Andhra Pradesh. Tel/Fax: (040) 27737145 Email: crystal_edwj@rediffmail.com

KENYA: Keswick Books and Gifts Ltd, PO Box 10242-00400, Nairobi.
Tel: (020) 2226047/312639 Email: sales.keswick@africaonline.co.ke

MALAYSIA: Canaanland, No. 25 Jalan PJU 1A/41B, NZX Commercial Centre, Ara Jaya, 47301 Petaling
Jaya, Selangor. Tel: (03) 7885 0540/1/2 Fax: (03) 7885 0545 Email: info@canaanland.com.my

Salvation Publishing & Distribution Sdn Bhd, 23 Jalan SS 2/64, 47300 Petaling Jaya, Selangor.
Tel: (03) 78766411/78766797 Fax: (03) 78757066/78756360 Email: info@salvationbookcentre.com

NEW ZEALAND: KI Entertainment, Unit 21 317-321 Woodpark Road, Smithfield, New South Wales
2164, Australia. Tel: 0 800 850 777 Fax: +612 9604 3699 Email: sales@kientertainment.com.au

NIGERIA: FBFM, Helen Baugh House, 96 St Finbarr's College Road, Akoka, Lagos.
Tel: (01) 7747429/4700218/825775/827264 Email: fbfm_1@yahoo.com

PHILIPPINES: OMF Literature Inc, 776 Boni Avenue, Mandaluyong City.
Tel: (02) 531 2183 Fax: (02) 531 1960 Email: gloadlaon@omflit.com

SINGAPORE: Alby Commercial Enterprises Pte Ltd, 95 Kallang Avenue #04-00, AIS Industrial Building,
339420. Tel: (65) 629 27238 Fax: (65) 629 27235 Email: marketing@alby.com.sg

SOUTH AFRICA: Struik Christian Media, 1st Floor, Wembley Square II, Solan Street, Gardens, Cape Town
8001, South Africa Tel: +27 (0) 21 460 5400 Fax: +27 (0) 21 461 7662 Email: info@struikchristianmedia.co.za

SRI LANKA: Christombu Publications (Pvt) Ltd, Bartleet House, 65 Braybrooke Place, Colombo 2.
Tel: (9411) 2421073/2447665 Email: dhanad@bartleet.com

USA: David C Cook Distribution Canada, PO Box 98, 55 Woodslee Avenue, Paris, Ontario N3L 3E5,
Canada. Tel: 1800 263 2664 Email: sandi.swanson@davidccook.ca

Cover to Cover Every Day

Gain deeper knowledge of the Bible

Each issue of these bimonthly daily Bible-reading notes gives you insightful commentary on a book of the Old and New Testaments with reflections on a psalm each weekend by Philip Greenslade.

Enjoy contributions from two well-known authors every two months, and over a five-year period you will be taken through the entire Bible.

 Individual issues available in print or epub/Kindle formats

Annual subscription available in print or via email.

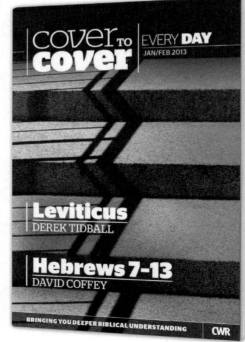

For current price or to order visit www.cwr.org.uk/store Available online or from Christian bookshops.

Cover to Cover Complete - NIV Edition
Read through the Bible chronologically

Take an exciting, year-long journey through the Bible, following events as they happened.

- See God's strategic plan of redemption unfold across the centuries
- Increase your confidence in the Bible as God's inspired message
- Come to know your heavenly Father in a deeper way

The full text of the flowing NIV provides an exhilarating reading experience and is augmented by our beautiful:

- Illustrations
- Maps
- Charts
- Diagrams
- Timeline

And key Scripture verses and devotional thoughts make each day's reading more meaningful.

ISBN: 978-1-85345-804-0

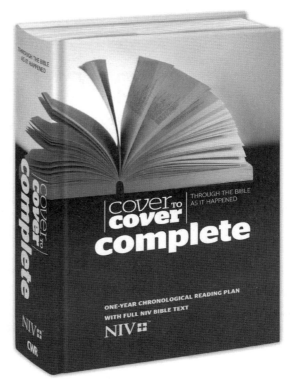

Courses and seminars

Publishing and new media

Conference facilities

Transforming lives

CWR's vision is to enable people to experience personal transformation through applying God's Word to their lives and relationships.

Our Bible-based training and resources help people around the world to:
• Grow in their walk with God
• Understand and apply Scripture to their lives
• Resource themselves and their church
• Develop pastoral care and counselling skills
• Train for leadership
• Strengthen relationships, marriage and family life and much more.

Our insightful writers provide daily Bible-reading notes and other resources for all ages, and our experienced course designers and presenters have gained an international reputation for excellence and effectiveness.

CWR's Training and Conference Centres in Surrey and West Sussex, England, provide excellent facilities in an idyllic setting – ideal for both learning and spiritual refreshment.

CWR Applying God's Word
to everyday life and relationships

CWR, Waverley Abbey House,
Waverley Lane, Farnham,
Surrey GU9 8EP, UK

Telephone: +44 (0)1252 784700
Email: info@cwr.org.uk
Website: www.cwr.org.uk

Registered Charity No 294387
Company Registration No 1990308